A CHIMPANZEE'S GUIDE FOR RETAIL MANAGEMENT

Bill Langston

authorHOUSE

AuthorHouse™
1663 Liberty Drive
Bloomington, IN 47403
www.authorhouse.com
Phone: 833-262-8899

© 2025 Bill Langston. All rights reserved.

No part of this book may be reproduced, stored in a retrieval system, or transmitted by any means without the written permission of the author.

Published by AuthorHouse 12/18/2024

ISBN: 979-8-8230-3953-6 (sc)
ISBN: 979-8-8230-3952-9 (hc)
ISBN: 979-8-8230-3951-2 (e)

Library of Congress Control Number: 2024926121

Print information available on the last page.

Any people depicted in stock imagery provided by Getty Images are models, and such images are being used for illustrative purposes only.
Certain stock imagery © Getty Images.

This book is printed on acid-free paper.

Because of the dynamic nature of the Internet, any web addresses or links contained in this book may have changed since publication and may no longer be valid. The views expressed in this work are solely those of the author and do not necessarily reflect the views of the publisher, and the publisher hereby disclaims any responsibility for them.

ASHLEY CRONMILLER
PHOTOGRAPHY
Cronmiller03@yahoo.com
Facebook: Ashley Cronmiller

Contents

FROM THE AUTHOR'S DESK; WHAT A CHIMP KNEEDS TO KNOW xi
INSPIRATION xiii
A UNIVERSAL TRUTH xv
DEDICATION xvii
A CHIMPANZEE'S GUIDE FOR RETAIL MANAGEMENT xix
GOOD ADVICE FOR THE MODERN CHIMP xxi

STORY 1	RETAIL CULTURE: A CHIMP'S COMMUNITY	1
STORY 2	GO AHEAD, MAKE MY DAY	3
STORY 3	DINASOURS, YOUNG LIONS AND HEADHUNTERS	5
STORY 4	MONKEY SEE, MONKEY DO; MY ATTITUDE, MY CONSIQUENCES	7
STORY 5	THE BAGBOY BLUES, WELCOME TO THE JUNGLE	9
STORY 6	HOW TO BATTLE A SUPERPOWER; RUN THROUGH THE JUNGLE	11
STORY 7	THE SCHEDULE: CHIMPS JUST WANT TO HAVE FUN	13
STORY 8	I LOVE WINNING; CHIMPS LOVE EXTRA BANANAS	15
STORY 9	WHAT THE HECK: KANGAROO COURT	17
STORY 10	A GOOD CHIMP NEVER BITES THE HAND THAT FEEDS HIM	19
STORY 11	LET THE CROOKS HAVE THE STORE; CHIMPS STAND DOWN	21

STORY 12	GO WITH YOUR GUT; ALL CHIMPS HAVE SPIDEY SENSES	23
STORY 13	YOU MAKE ME SMILE; AND A CHIMP LOVES TO SMILE	25
STORY 14	STOCK CREW SHANNANIGANS; CHIMPS GONE WILD	29
STORY 15	CHRONIC TARDY SYNDROM; MAKES A CHIMP INCOMPITENT	35
STORY 16	ANGER IS A GOOD CHIMPS ENEMY	37
STORY 17	MR. PERFECT: NO CHIMP IS PERFECT	39
STORY 18	NO WORRIES, MATE: CHIMPS DON'T FREAK OUT	41
STORY 19	CHANGE IS A FACT OF LIFE; CHIMPS MUST ADAPT	43
STORY 20	THE WELL-DRESSED CHIMP	45
STORY 21	PAPA CHIMP ALWAYS GUARDS THE COMMUNITY	47
STORY 22	STAY ON SCRIPT, BUT I WANT MORE! WHAT'S HAPPENING CHIMPS	49
STORY 23	KEEPER OF THE GATE; CHIMPS TAKING CARE OF BUSINESS	51
STORY 24	CUSTOMER SERVICE MANAGER, HEADCASHIER, MAMA CHIMP	53
STORY 25	DON'T BE A SEAGULL; SMART CHIMPS KNOW HOW TO BE A LEADER	55
STORY 26	BEST JOB IN THE STORE; CHIMPS IN THE FAST LANE	57
STORY 27	RED ALERT; BATTLE STATIONS...... DOUBLE COUPONS	59
STORY 28	COOKIE MONSTERS AND MILE HIGH KEY LIME PIE	61
STORY 29	MOONLIGHT MADNESS OR WILD WEDNESDAY SALES	63
STORY 30	CLEANUP ON AISLE SIX; CHIMPS HATE TO CLEAN UP A MESS	65

STORY 31	THIS IS MY STORE; SMART CHIMPS TAKE OWNERSHIP	67
STORY 32	PREPARING FOR THE STORM; STAY SAFE CHIMPS	69
STORY 33	THE ALPHA	73
STORY 34	THE ANGEL OF DEATH	75
STORY 35	SOMETHING NEW	77
STORY 36	MY WORKING FAMILY	79

ACKNOWLEDGMENTS 81

FROM THE AUTHOR'S DESK; WHAT A CHIMP KNEEDS TO KNOW

A Chimpanzee's guide for retail management was written from the author's point of view, your point of view may differ. The content offers no promises or guarantees. These are short stories of my own experiences intermingled with advice I received over the years. Sometimes it was trial and error on my part but at the end, this is what worked for me during my retail management career.

Very few people are lucky enough to find the perfect job. Even if you happen to find your dream job, it usually comes with attachments you may not like or co-workers and bosses you, for some reason or another, just can't get along with.

Some people hate working in retail and had rather stand in an unemployment line than accept a position in any store. However, for myself and many of my acquaintances, we have enjoyed a fulfilling career in retail. I know bagboys that climbed the ladder of success all the way to VP or Regional Director even to become the CEO.

IF YOU WANT IT, THE SKY IS THE LIMIT.

INSPIRATION

In my opinion the most important key for success is Inspiration. To be inspired to reach new and higher goals. The inner desire to be the best. A hunger that keeps you motivated and driven to be the best version of you.

A UNIVERSAL TRUTH

If you don't get your ass out of bed in the morning and go do it, it isn't going to get done.

The world doesn't owe you a damn thing.

DEDICATION

During my career in retail, I have had many bosses. There is one boss that stands above all the others, Mr. Leon Stewart. He was more than my boss; he was my mentor but most importantly he was my friend. Mr. Stewart never hesitated to tell you like it was, whether it hurt your feelings or not. But if you truly listened it made you a better manager or even a better person.

Mr. Stewart was one of those bosses that always had your back even if it meant taking heat from upper management to defend your good name. If he believed in you, he would stand by your side regardless of whatever the odds may be. No problem was ever too big or too small, he was always there to help.

Mr. Stewart's district won it all, there wasn't a challenge we could not conquer, no goals, no quotas and milestones that stood in our way. We set the pace, we set the standard for all others to follow. He led by example, showing hard work and commitment always paid off.

I will forever remember the year end parties we had at his home and the countless times he took our district and our spouses out for dinner. It was a chance to let our hair down and howl at the moon. It took us away from the everyday problems we faced as managers and built unity in our district. We were his band of brothers. We were Stewart's Stompers.

Thank you, Mr. Stewart, for all the things you did for me and my family, we will be forever grateful.

A CHIMPANZEE'S GUIDE FOR RETAIL MANAGEMENT

FORWARD

During my forty-three years in retail, forty-one of them were in management. At the end of one of my walks through the store with a VP of our company he passed along to me some of the best and most profound compliments I would ever receive. He was happy with the store's conditions, happy with bottom-line profit results, increased sales results, recent inventory results and informed me the store walk had made his day.

"You know something Bill"? "You make operating a store look so easy a Chimpanzee could do it". "You have surrounded yourself with good, hard working, competent people that have made your job look easy". And that my friend is the key to my success, surround myself with the best of the best. Thank you, Mr. Howard Hess.

Surrounding myself with good people made my working life so much easier which in turn made my personal life a happy life.

GOOD ADVICE FOR THE MODERN CHIMP

I   NEVER LET MONEY BE YOUR ONLY MOTIVATOR
II   KEEP YOUR FAMILY AS YOUR NUMBER ONE PRIORITY
III   TREAT YOUR ASSOCIATES WITH RESPECT
IV   BE OPEN MINDED FOR NEW IDEAS
V   NEVER LIE, CHEAT OR STEAL
VI   LISTEN TO YOUR CUSTOMERS AND YOUR ASSOCIATES
VII   BUILD PRIDE IN ALL YOU DO
VIII   ALWAYS MAKE IT RIGHT
XI   BE A GOOD COMMUNICATOR AND MOTIVATOR
X   SHARE THE WEALTH
XI   YOU ARE ONLY AS GOOD AS YOUR PEOPLE
XII   IF YOU NEVER TRY, YOU NEVER KNOW
XIII   ALWAYS DO YOUR BEST
XIV   TOMORROW IS A NEW DAY
XV   IF YOU'RE NOT TEN MINUTES EARLY, YOU'RE LATE
XVI   LOOK SHARP, DRESS SHARP, BE SHARP

STORY 1

RETAIL CULTURE: A CHIMP'S COMMUNITY

It doesn't matter what type of retail establishment you are affiliated with they all have many things in common, yet they are different. It could be a restaurant, a department store, a gas station, even a convenience store or grocery store, they all have their own culture, their own place in retail.

A retail establishment is like a mini city. They have their own mayor, AKA store manager, their own city council AKA assistants or department heads. They also have their own citizens, employees that show up for work every day. These establishments also have their own government AKA corporate, giving them a set of rules to live their working lives by.

In return for their hard work the community's mayor, councilmen and citizens are paid with a weekly or biweekly check, sometimes overtime, bonuses, 401K retirement plan, vacations, insurance and other special incentives.

The community has common goals like making money in the form of profits for whatever entity they are a part of. Delivering good customer service, keeping a clean well stocked store. Merchandising for the customers' needs is also a high priority.

One's social life may also revolve around work friends and community events. Most employees like to hang out after work or meet for some other social gathering.

If you were to park your car down the street from any retail store you would observe the fact it was like a beehive or an ant hill. The workers busying themselves taking care of corporate business.

STORY 2

GO AHEAD, MAKE MY DAY

I arrive at the store an hour before opening time so I can check all departments before the first customer enters the store. My crew is already there and has been working hard for the past few hours waiting for my seal of approval. The first thing I notice is how clean the floors are. Freshly waxed and buffed I can see my smile in the reflection on the floor as I start to make my way around the store.

Beauty is in the eye of the beholder especially when it comes to the grocery business. To a true grocery man there is nothing more beautiful than a well-stocked grocery store. Ones whose aisles are perfectly finessed as if the product is standing at attention, like soldiers, waiting for inspection. All labels facing out forming a straight line down the entire length of the aisle. An aisle that looks like an artist had just finished painting a perfect picture. Rows of aisles perfectly finessed reflecting pride in its workers and waiting for customers to admire in "awe", the beauty it radiates.

A perishable department exploding with freshness as if the perfect garden had somehow manifested itself into the four walls of my store. And a meat department full of freshly cut meats shouting "it's Bar B Que time" so loudly the sound is almost deafening. The smell of fresh baked bread gives me the feeling that I'm home.

To make it the perfect store, my employees are at their assigned stations, clean and neat, ready to shmooze customers with first-class service as they walk in the front doors. Ready to "WOW" the most sinical of clients.

STORY 3

DINASOURS, YOUNG LIONS AND HEADHUNTERS

Countless things have changed since my first management position as an eighteen-year-old. Fresh out of high school, full of piss and vinegar, ready to grab the world by the tail. The year was nineteen seventy and I was eager to throw my hat into the management arena, ready to show the big bosses that I was worthy to take the helm of my own store.

Today I would be a dinosaur in a land filled with young lions. Being a taskmaster, order giver, schedule maker and organizer wouldn't be enough. I would need computer skills, diversity training, sexual harassment training, accepting change training and whatever other training the powers of upper management feel a manager needs to survive in today's retail climate.

After forty plus years in retail management, most of them in the grocery business, I find myself finessing aisles and picking items up off the floor to put in their place on the shelf every time I go shopping. I find myself double checking dates and being judgmental of a stores appearance and what I would do better. I find myself wondering why that employee doesn't have a nametag or why is that person in a position of customer service with an attitude of a charging rhinoceros or wounded water buffalo. I wonder why I always grab a shopping cart or two from the parking lot on my way into a store. I guess it's in the blood or old habits are hard to break.

With management positions in high demand more than ever before, companies are quick to go to other companies to recruit management. Headhunters get paid big bucks to find members of management ready to jump ship and take a position with whatever company that hired them to find you. I too have been stalked by headhunters hoping to get me to switch companies with very lucrative offers. The only reason I didn't accept their offers was I didn't want to relocate to a big city or drive more than an hour to get to my new job.

Promotion through the ranks is almost a thing of the past with corporations looking for college degrees or managers that already have experience. Working for more the four large corporations in a management position I discovered a few intangibles that headhunters or companies seeking experienced managers couldn't bring to the table. True loyalty, pride and comradery are meaningful intangibles that are so much stronger when you earn them.

When an individual starts at the bottom and works their way up the ladder of success comes an intangible called loyalty. True loyalty isn't something you can put a price on, and neither is pride. Both these intangibles are stronger when you earn them than when they are bought and paid for and are expected by your employer. It's like a teenager and his first car. When he earns the money and pays for it him or herself, they are more proud of it than if it were given to them by mom and dad.

STORY 4

MONKEY SEE, MONKEY DO; MY ATTITUDE, MY CONSIQUENCES

This entity we call attitude is the driving force behind excitement, enthusiasm, pride, courage, determination and willpower. Attitude makes things happen. The attitude one has is usually the deciding factor in most of life's challenges. A positive attitude ultimately wins the battle as there is no substitute for a positive attitude. It can be as contagious as excitement and can have more worth than experience. A positive attitude is rarely defeated and knows no boundaries.

To harness this entity, we call positive attitude and use its positive powers in one's organization is not a mystery. It starts with the leader as he sets the pace. If the leader doesn't always have a positive attitude, it is looked upon as a weakness to his peers. Regardless of the leader's task it must be conveyed with a positive attitude to get the best results. Anything less creates doubt in the minds of those dependent upon executing plans to achieve the desired results.

The common denominator amongst all great leaders is their positive attitude, their cando spirit. Whether it be a leader in sports, government, a leader on the battlefield or industry, their positive attitude always stood out like a shining star.

Anyway you want to look at it, sales is an attitude. If you don't have a sales mentality, coupled with a positive attitude, you may never reach the paramount of sales you are looking for.

STORY 5

THE BAGBOY BLUES, WELCOME TO THE JUNGLE

I was ready to quit, to throw in the towel or just plain walk off the job after only a few hours. It wasn't because of rude customers, separating soda bottles in the bottle room, cleaning the restrooms or even sweeping the store. But gathering shopping carts when the parking lot is on the side of a hill, just about killed me.

It seemed like every customer that shopped in the store took sport in rolling their empty cart down the hill where they merged into a tangled mass. After only a few hours at my new bagboy job, which I really liked, the manager sent me out into the parking lot to collect shopping carts as there were none left in the store.

Walking down the hill until I reached the bottom seemed like an all-day Army hike. A hike in double-time where loud mouthed sergeants yelled cadence at the top of their lungs. To make matters worse it was July in Florida, and the temperature was pushing triple digits. I could feel the sweat making its way in streams down my entire body into my new shoes that were already rubbing a blister on my heel. My clean, freshly pressed white shirt was so wet with sweat it looked as though I had fallen into the nearby retention pond near the mass of shopping carts.

After about a half an hour all the carts were relocated into the store and the manager took pity upon me, sending me on a fifteen-minute break. I was exhausted and needed it more than the manager could imagine.

I headed straight to the water fountain where I quenched my thirst and then to the breakroom where I sat for the rest of my break. I felt good, after all I just got paid for fifteen minutes that I spent sitting on my butt. I wasn't used to taking a break and had never taken one at any other job before this. That's the minute I decided to stay. That $1.60 per hour I was getting paid seemed like a lot of money at the time. Not to mention the five dollars I had made in tips that afternoon was like free money.

The rest of the week was better, and I had gotten used to gathering the shopping carts at the bottom of the hill. I had also decided the maroon bowtie issued to me wasn't all that bad either.

When my first Saturday at work arrived, by the end of my shift my pockets were so full of quarters they couldn't hold anymore. I went to the office and traded them for paper money. WOW! More than twenty-five dollars in tips. That was more than I was paid for my eight hours' work. Once a lady's car trunk was full of empty soda bottles and she asked if I would like to have them. Yes, I filled two shopping carts full of empty bottles and to my surprise when I cashed them in there was almost twenty dollars. What a tip.

Life was good and getting better.

STORY 6

HOW TO BATTLE A SUPERPOWER; RUN THROUGH THE JUNGLE

The pros and cons of a Walmart Supercenter, Target or any other industry giant opening in a small town can be debated for hours with no true victor. Sure, it creates more jobs for the community, brings in more tax revenue while encouraging growth. But for every job it creates how many small businesses must close their doors, lay off employees or cut their hours? Sounds like a catch 22 doesn't it.

When a construction sign for any industry giant is placed in an area you can rest assured it will most likely be built. Regardless of protest, restrictions, wildlife concerns, setbacks or whatever community problems may arise, they have the money and power to fix it. I honestly hope the business community in these small towns will be prepared for the impact these giants will have on the small business owner.

Below are ten tips to help the small businessman in his quest to keep customers and build sales.

1. Is your staff customer service conscious and sales driven
   If not, train and lead them because customers and sales can be won with the best customer service in town.
2. Are your customers your friend? If not, make them, as a bond of friendship will pay big dividends in your quest for sales?
3. Include the community in many of your store's events. After all, you were there first and the community looks up to you for support of many of its projects.

4. Have fun with your customers and associates; make your business the place to be. Popular places don't just happen, make your business a popular hot spot for working, shopping or dining.
5. If a customer forgets an item in your store, exhaust all means of finding that person and let them know if they like you will take it to them. They will appreciate the special attention.
6. If there is a complaint, make it right. Even if you lose a little money, you still win by making the customer happy.
7. Make it clear for your associates to NEVER SAY NO to your customers. Make the decision to say NO strictly a management decision.
8. If your product isn't top notch, make it top notch. Make it top notch, as there is no substitute for quality. Especially if your business is in the food industry.
9. Cleanliness is next to Godliness, especially in the eyes of your customers. It should be the same way with you and your staff.
10. Do not let payroll, expenses or man hours be a stumbling block. Your reputation is at risk. To your customers, their perception of you and your associates is everything. Do not let your customers down, make sure they leave your business HAPPY.

Whether you're a small hometown business or a large corporation there is no substitute for excellent customer service. If your prices are anywhere near competitive and the quality of your product is as good as your competitors', just put the frosting on the cake with the best service in town.

Remember above all else, everyone that walks through the front door of your business is a special person, a guest in your home and ultimately your friend. They could have chosen to shop or dine anywhere but they have chosen to be at your place. Don't let them down.

STORY 7

THE SCHEDULE: CHIMPS JUST WANT TO HAVE FUN

I always hated making work schedules. There was always someone that complained about not enough hours or I don't want to work that day or that shift. When you missed someone's request for time off or couldn't fill it in for some reason, they took it personally. In any event there were those that were not happy with anything you try to do. The hardest job in the store is to make a schedule that makes everyone happy.

Making a schedule always seemed like doing homework and I would put it off until the last minute or do parts of it a little at a time. Did I mention I hated making schedules?

After a few years in management, I came up with a master plan. Post a calendar in the office for all to write their name on whatever day they needed or wanted off and give it to them regardless. This meant I needed to hire extra personnel so that I was never in a bind for help.

I had a store meeting and introduced my calendar letting everyone know I didn't care what days you wanted off but for it to work, if you were scheduled you had better be at work unless it were a big-time emergency. I also informed the older staff that when prom, homecoming, graduation or any other school event happened they would need to be available to work one of those nights. I also informed everyone if they are calling in sick, they needed to call in two hours before their shift or preferably call the night before. This way it was easier to cover their shift. Did I mention I hated making schedules?

Everyone took advantage of the calendar concept. I hired more staff, and the most amazing thing is the call outs were almost nonexistent. I guess the O'Jays had it right, give the people what they want.

STORY 8

I LOVE WINNING; CHIMPS LOVE EXTRA BANANAS

People in other professions don't believe how competitive and lucrative a career in retail can be. It's unbelievable how many contests and incentives are created to inspire its management teams to reach new heights in sales and profits.

Many industries have an incentive program second to none. Great bonus programs, monthly sales incentives, quarterly sales bonuses, department display contest, steak and bean dinners complete with door prizes where the winners eat steak and the losers try to choke down a plate of pork and beans along with their pride, but all in good fun. To top it off they have great retirement programs such as profit sharing and 401K incentives.

As a store manager I took a page out of the corporate playbook creating my own in-store incentives, motivating my employees with prizes for a job well done. I even dubbed my stock crew as the Super Crew. They did a Super job day in and day out, ensuring the store was well stocked.

We received grocery trucks three days a week and on those days the stock crew pulled an all nightery. At nine p.m. on those nights, I would come into the store and call the crew together. We put everyone's name into a hat drawing two names as potential nightly winners for the perfect aisle. The entire crew, an assistant and I would go to the two winner's aisles and critique them. We were looking for clean shelves, proper placement of shelf tags, no damaged merchandise on display, shelf skyline observed and no over stocking. About every two weeks the perfect aisle was found and the winner received movie tickets, ball game tickets, a gift card to their favorite restaurant or some other gift of their choosing. In any case they were winning, and I was winning and ultimately the customer was winning.

I shouldn't forget to include my cashiers as the winning team. After all they are the lifeblood of your business and are usually the only person a customer may encounter while shopping in your store. They are your store's best form of good public relations. So, the Five for Lunch Bunch was formed. The top performing cashiers for a four-week period were invited to lunch with me paying for wherever they wanted to eat, at whatever restaurant they chose.

The Five for Lunch, Bunch contest rules were simple. How well the cashier's till balanced daily, most rings per minute, attendance and their mystery shopper scores. Taking all five cashiers to lunch was the best way to celebrate the best cashiers in town.

I love winning display contests, I love winning sales contests and eating steak at our steak and bean dinners. I love winning so anytime the word contest is mentioned it's GAME ON!

STORY 9

WHAT THE HECK: KANGAROO COURT

Shoplifting always has been a problem in retail stores. However, the treatment of those that chose to become retail thieves during the sixties and seventies was surely a lot harsher than today.

When I was a sixteen-year-old bagboy my store manager had his own method for prosecuting those that chose to steal from his store. The severity of the punishment depended upon several elements. The first being what items had they chosen to steal, secondly why had they taken it, were they trying to feed their family, was it medicine for a sick child, or they just wanted it. Last on the list was how old was the culprit.

One Saturday morning, several elementary-age school kids (all boys) parked their bicycles in front of the store. When they entered the store they went straight to the candy aisle, filling their pockets with as much candy as they could jam into their pockets. When they looked up the boss was standing at one end of the aisle and two more clerks were waiting for them at the other end. The manager escorted the captured villains to the backroom and on to the ice cream freezer. The manager lectured them for several minutes about stealing before having the frightened kids remove their shoes and socks. Their punishment was standing, barefoot, in the ice cream freezer for thirty seconds with the lights off. When the freezer door was opened the kids were dancing and promising to never steal again. Today the manager and those helping would be charged with child abuse and probably several other charges.

If the parents had been called to come to the store and get their kids for shoplifting undoubtedly the punishment, they would have received at home would have been worse than thirty seconds, barefoot, in the ice cream freezer. In those days parents didn't put up with bad behavior.

Usually when a shoplifter was captured, they were escorted to the backroom to wait for the police department to arrive. Depending upon the shoplifter's attitude Kangaroo court might be held. If they were combative, abusive or just plain arrogant, Kangaroo court was in session. All the management team, department heads and any available employees were called to the backroom where they circled the accused thief. Each person had the opportunity to confront the thief at that point, scolding or cursing the villain, making sure he got the message, you don't steal from our store family.

Young mothers stealing medication for a sick baby, an elderly person with no money to buy food or even a homeless person were forgiven and usually left the store with the item they took at no charge.

I could write an entire book about shoplifters and the chase to see that justice was served. I've seen a whole turkey smuggled out of the store between a lady's thighs, I've seen mop crews hide product in their scrubbing machine, people run out the front doors with a shopping cart full of meat. I've seen people bring their own shopping bags into the store filling them with product trying to pass it off as if they had paid for it. I've been on high-speed chases, chasing a young couple that stole a quart of chocolate milk. A police officer and I even chased a man that stole two twelve packs of beer down the sidewalk.

I have also had compassion for those stealing from the store. I once bought groceries for a woman that had stolen Tylenol for her sick dad. They had no food in the house, and I made sure they had enough groceries for a week. Sometimes you just have to help.

STORY 10

A GOOD CHIMP NEVER BITES THE HAND THAT FEEDS HIM

Employee theft is much greater than the public realizes. Companies spend millions of dollars trying to stop employee theft as it eats away more profits than shoplifting ever did.

Surveillance cameras aren't just there to detour shoplifters they are positioned so big brother can keep tabs on its employees. Cameras are positioned in the office, above every cash register and over every front and back entrance/exit to the store. They are in every aisle and every department. The cameras produce evidence for slip and fall claims and product tampering. Surveillance cameras have saved companies billions of dollars in lawsuits over the years. I believe cameras are everywhere in retail stores except restrooms.

Before cameras you had to depend upon conscientious employees keeping management in the know when something underhanded was going on. Sometimes it was just plain luck catching the thieves or following company security guidelines always paid off.

It isn't pretty when you catch an employee stealing. Someone you trusted to be honest.

I've caught bagboys handing off cartons of cigarettes to friends to smuggle out of the store. I've had young cashiers set wine coolers beside the front doors for an outside source to grab and run to a waiting car full of friends and cases of beer stolen the same way.

Other employees trying to get a cashier friend to only ring up a few items of a whole basket of groceries. One teenage cashier tried paying off his drug dealer by having the dealer go through his line and not ring anything up at all.

During one store grand opening the computers that run the front-end cash registers kept sporadically going offline causing daily balancing of the tills almost impossible for an entire week. A young office girl took advantage of the problem and was stealing as much as twelve hundred dollars a day. One of my senior citizen bagboys informed me he saw an office girl grab a handful of money from an unattended register, place it into a small bag and hide said money in the checkout stand under the register. I removed the bag and

called the corporate loss prevention department. During the investigation she admitted stealing over ten thousand dollars. Catching her was only by luck and the actions of an honest employee.

It always made me angry when I caught one of my employees stealing from me. I could never understand how someone could steal from a company that put food on their table and a roof over their head. Never bite the hand that feeds you.

STORY 11

LET THE CROOKS HAVE THE STORE; CHIMPS STAND DOWN

Give the crooks what they want because there is nothing in the store worth yours or anyone else's life. If they want money, tell them you will be happy to double bag it and carry it to the car for them if nobody gets hurt.

During my retail career I have chased shoplifters, purse snatchers and strong-armed robbers behind the store to retrieve the store's merchandise or a customer's purse. When I look back today, I realize how stupid I was to put my life at risk. It would have been much wiser for me to have let law enforcement do their job, after all I wasn't trained to apprehend criminals.

I've had friends pistol whipped and made to open the safe. Friends threatened with both guns and knives and crooks waiting in the parking lot to ambush them. Some crooks went as far as hiding in the restrooms until the store closed and everyone had gone home so they could take whatever they chose.

I've been very lucky as my store was never robbed at gunpoint but several of my neighboring stores were not so lucky. Threesomes of crooks were targeting large stores in my area. The driver would stay in the car, keeping it running and ready to flee the scene. One would go to the office with a shotgun demanding the safe be opened while the third kept look out. They got away with robbing a few stores, but their luck ran out.

When they were holding-up a store in Leesburg Florida, the lookout stuck his 357 magnum into the front of his pants. When exiting the store, he tripped causing the gun to fire, blowing off his testicals. Which in turn scared the driver causing him to leave his two accomplices behind. The shotgun carrying member ran behind the store where he had a shootout with the local police department. He didn't make it.

My advice to you if you are ever threatened at gun point or with any other weapon, STAY CALM, but give the crooks what they want. Your safety and the people with you, comes first.

STORY 12

GO WITH YOUR GUT; ALL CHIMPS HAVE SPIDEY SENSES

You might laugh or even shake your head, but Spidey Senses are a real thing. Everyone is born with a sixth sense commonly known as a gut feeling or intuition.

I've always had the ability to sense some things before they happen or know that someone wasn't telling me the truth or even foresee or predict danger before it happens. During this chapter I will share with you some of the times my Spidey Senses came in handy.

I had been a store manager for only two months when my Spidey senses started tingling on Thanksgiving morning. The store was closed, and my family and I were just about to leave the house to go out of town to have Thanksgiving with relatives. The phone rang and the voice on the other end was a complaint that my store had ruined their Thanksgiving because the turkey they bought was bad. The man was forceful and demanded I meet him at the store so he could get another turkey. (Back then Store managers had their phone number displayed in the front window with other emergency numbers) Spidey senses kick in and I knew it was a hoax and told the caller that the police department and I would be there in thirty minutes that I couldn't go into the store by myself. I never went to the store.

Spidey Senses incident number two. In our area four or five hoodlums would come into the store, split up, and cause a distraction so one or two of them could grab money from an unsuspecting cashier while her till was open, and run out of the store. I saw the five young men come into the store and I instantly knew what they were up to. I quickly walked over to the leader and acted as if I knew him. I asked if he was still playing football and told him how much I enjoyed watching him play. I also asked how his mom was doing and I hoped to see her soon. The leader smiled and said he hadn't played for a while and his mom was doing well. He signaled the others, and they all walked out of the store with none of our money and no merchandise.

Spidey Senses incident number three. A young stock clerk I was cross training on a cash register had only run his till for maybe ten minutes total during his shift. When it was time to check out his till was $100.00 short exactly. He had only cashed one check, and it was for two hundred plus dollars. Immediately I knew he had given the extra money to whoever had cashed the check. I called the phone number on the back and the man that cashed it refused to come in and bring the money back. He denied that it ever happened. I told the young clerk that we were going to have to make the man think that I was going to fire him if he didn't bring the money back.

I had the clerk call the man appealing to his sense of fair play and that I was going to fire him if we didn't get the money back. Within minutes the man came back to the store to set me straight and appeal for the clerk's job. Still denying he had gotten the extra money.

Before the man got back to the store, I had told the young clerk to go along with whatever I said, and we would get together after the man left the store.

With my clerk and the man standing there I asked again if he had gotten the extra money, again he denied it. So, I acted like I was angry, even ripping off my clip-on tie and throwing it on the floor. I yelled at the clerk in front of the man, "if you don't give me the hundred dollars, you're fired." Then I walked away in a huff.

The man and my clerk walked out of the store together and in a few short minutes the clerk returned with a smile on his face and the store's $100.00 in his hand. (The envelope given to the customer had $100.00 marker on it, however the envelope contained $200.00)

Those are only a few instances where my Spidey Senses paid off and over the years they helped me on many occasions. I discovered the longer I was a store manager the more valuable my Spidey Senses became.

STORY 13

YOU MAKE ME SMILE; AND A CHIMP LOVES TO SMILE

Like most people I like to reflect upon my working days. I smile when I think about working at Winn-Dixie during the sixties, seventies and eighties. Those were magical years when all things were possible.

I smile when I think about all the friendships I made while working there and even after more than five decades we remain friends. I smile when I think about the bond we will always share.

I like to remember going shopping at Kwik Chek with my mom when I was a preschooler and her filling the shopping cart to where it overflowed, using her fifteen dollar a week grocery budget. And I smile remembering my Lucas McCain "The Rifleman" rifle, she got with TV stamps, for my birthday.

The Orlando division, AKA The Big O, was a new addition to the Winn-Dixie family in the early seventies and I smile when I remember a young Dan Lafever, Hal Klopper, Ken Clack, Howard Hess, Tom Mathews, Mike Cornish, Roy Fountain, Mike Prugh, Elio Florin, Richard Sturgill, Dan Wynn, Chip DeClue, Ron Murphy, Homer Ryan, Ron Crabtree, Dennis Bantz, John Few, Duane Finch, Tom Goolsby, Virgil Screws and Jere Bedford. It made me smile watching them climb the ladder of success and achieve many goals.

I smile when I remember old timers like Luther Hipps, Roy Holmes, John Wynn, Ellis Ware, Albert Shaw, A.C. Bracher, Billy Wells, Sam Evans, Leon Stewart, Al Davis, Jim Kufeldt, Bernard Webb and Roy and Carter Gudal.

Gary Finch and Billy Wells hired me as a sixteen-year-old bagboy. And I smile when I remember my first day at work and how nervous I was. I smile when I remember Gary Finch taking his time showing me around the store, introducing me as the new guy to my fellow workers. I remember how patient he was when teaching how to bag groceries and explaining what a bagboys duty was. A few weeks later he promoted me to the stock crew.

Charlie McKellar was a no-nonsense kind of guy and usually worked your store hard. During the seventies and eighties if you got a call from a fellow store manager saying he just had "A BIG MAC ATTACK" he wasn't referring to a visit to the local McDonalds. Charlie McKellar had just left his store. I also smile and even laugh about one of his visits to my store. I had a Tampax display at the end of the candy aisle, and he was quick to tell me, "I know people eat candy and people eat snatch, but that tampon display doesn't belong there". We laughed and moved the display. If you listened, he did have a great sense of humor.

I smile when I remember my rise from bagboy to store manager and all the hard work it took to get there.

I smile when I think about our steak and bean dinners during the seventies and eighties and what great fun they were. I remember us Eagles losing to the Cougars on a rematch and having to eat crow for the first and only time as a store manager. I even wrote Dan Lafever a song to play after we had our dessert. A local country western band put it to music and recorded it on a cassette tape. (The Cougars referred to us Eagles as Disco Ducks)

WE DON'T LIKE DISCO DUCK

We don't like disco duck, and we don't like pork and beans.
We don't like losing, we don't know what it means.
This old bird might have stumbled but he ain't ever fell,
And if the cougars don't like it, they can all go straight to hell!

That's all I can remember of the song, but the country western band put it to the tune of The Wabash Cannonball. You gotta laugh and smile when you think about those days and how magical they were. The friendly competition between stores and their management teams is just one of the small things that turn out to be great memories.

I smile but miss the fact that we closed every Sunday and every holiday, I can remember when Dan Lafever and Ken Clack had hair, John McDaniels hair was still black, and Tom Mathews was my market manager. I still remember making orders out on paper and hurrying to get it on the Greyhound bus so the warehouse would receive our orders on time. I smile when I remember a wise old Luther Hipps still on top of his game. I smile when I think about us country boys going to an Orlando divisional meeting and afterwards having a night out on the town.

Mr. Kufeldt was mild mannered and never lost his temper with myself or my fellow store managers and that makes me smile. He was wise and looked at everything from the customer's point of view. I smile when I think about John Wynn's booming voice and how efficient he was getting a store reset or a new store ready for its grand opening.

I smile when I remember Rich Ester, our Division Manager, coming to my store after I put in my resignation. He was concerned about my leaving and asked if there was anything he could do to influence me to stay. That made me feel important.

I smile when I think about Jenelle Lott, Bob Blakely and Ken Clack, knowing if I had a problem, they were only a phone call away. They were the "A" team.

I smile when I remember baseball great Roger Maris visiting my store with his route man. I thought he was a trainee and had him clean shelves and move displays! I didn't know who he was and didn't know that the Budweiser franchise out of Ocala and Gainesville belonged to him. He did everything I asked without saying a word.

I smile when I remember my old produce manager Jimmy "RED SOCKS" Hanson and what a great produce team he and his crew were. Number one in produce gross profit in both Tampa and the Orlando divisions for many years.

Not every day was perfect during my career in retail, but I choose not to dwell on those and focus on the good ones. Because they far outnumber any of the bad days I might have had. Having worked for three other grocery chains I can honestly say none compared to how well Winn-Dixie treated its management team.

STORY 14

STOCK CREW SHANNANIGANS; CHIMPS GONE WILD

At one time practical jokes were a daily occurrence in retail life. Having a good sense of humor was almost mandatory. With today's standards forget about playing practical jokes on your co-workers as there are way too many rules and too many people get their feelings hurt and will file a complaint.

Some practical jokes are simple like sending a new clerk for a shelf stretcher or sky hook. Imitating the voice of your VP, calling neighboring stores, giving them orders or requesting confidential sales information. Or sending a bagboy to the office for a masturbation application when he is requesting a promotion to the stock crew. Then there are practical jokes that go to extremes. The practical jokes I'm writing about really happened and some folks still laugh about them today.

JOKE #1......IT'S 5 O'CLOCK SOMEWHERE

There is nothing better than an ice-cold beer at the end of a long workday. Especially if you have just finished a ten-to-twelve-hour shift.

One manager, every night he closed the store, placed a twelve pack of his favorite beer in the freezer spot case or the ice cream case about a half an hour before he left to go home. By then the beer was so cold it had formed little ice crystals.

Knowing this a clerk waited and took the beer to a sink in the back where he removed a can from the package. He made a hole in the bottom of the can and replaced the beer with salt water. He then sealed the can and package as if nothing ever happened and put the beer back in the freezer.

A few days passed and the manager, the clerk and several peers were having lunch in the breakroom. The clerk casually states: "I heard on the news last night the brewery was recalling your favorite beer as someone was urinating in the cans"! The manager gasps, "OH NO, I think I got one"! The breakroom filled with laughter, and I believe the clerk is still laughing!

JOKE #2......STAY FRESH

The meat department manager at one of the fifteen stores I had managed loved to flirt with the lady customers. He kept a bottle of cologne in his desk drawer and would splash a little on several times during the day and always refreshed himself after lunch.

The manager was giving a young part-time produce clerk a rough time for weeks and the clerk felt it was time to retaliate. The next time the manager went to lunch the clerk went into his desk and took the bottle of cologne. He headed to the restroom where he emptied the entire bottle into the sink, refilling it with his own urine!

When the manager returned, he went straight to his desk, grabbed the bottle of cologne, filled the palm of his hand and splashed it onto his face. ROGERRRRRR!!!! (not his real name) the manager screamed at the top of his lungs knowing instantly who had replaced his cologne with piss!!

And the chase began, as the manager chased Roger out of the store into the street and down the block. The manager returned without Roger and headed to the restroom where he washed his face several times before returning to work. I sent Roger home for the remainder of the day it just wasn't safe for him to come back into the store.

JOKE #3......GEORGE'S SHIRT

At one time all the male workers were required to wear a white shirt and tie to work. The stock crew was no exception. After the store closed the crew would take their shirt and tie off because it was way more comfortable stocking in one's t-shirt or no shirt. And from time to time someone's shirt would be hidden as a prank.

When George was pranked, they didn't just hide his shirt, it was taken to the mop sink where it was soaked with water then put on a clothes hanger and hung in the walk-in freezer.

George worked hard all night and when it was time to go, he was shirtless, looking everywhere his shirt might be, it was nowhere to be found. Finally, someone says, "have you looked in the coolers or freezers"? There it was, hanging in the back of the freezer, his shirt was a solid sheet of ice! You could hear George yelling all the way to the front of the store. It was a good thing we hadn't opened yet as customers might have thought someone was being murdered in the backroom.

JOKE #4……Oh crap, not an STD!!!

When you are pranking your friends, you must always be aware of retaliation. It might not be immediate, but you know in the back of your mind sooner or later it is going to happen.

One of my good-natured assistant managers use to like to pull the occasional practical joke on his subordinates and they retaliated in a big way.

While he and I were doing paperwork in my office the phone rang. I answered like usual and the voice on the other end wanted to speak to my assistant. I handed him the phone and kept busy doing paperwork.

"No, no way, that isn't true" I heard my assistant's voice quivering. He was also turning kind of pale and saying a lot of yes sirs to whoever was on the other end of the conversation.

"I have to talk to you, that was a Dr. Welch from the county health department". "He said my girlfriend has an STD". "He also said I have thirty minutes to get to his office and if I

didn't get there, he was sending a deputy sheriff to pick me up". After a few minutes passed he reluctantly left to meet DR Welch.

At the health department he approached the front desk, "I'm here to see Dr. Welch", he stated to the two-lady receptionist. "There is no Dr Welch here". In a panic he explained his dilemma, that he was told his girlfriend had an STD and to get there immediately.

The receptionist is still laughing.

JOKE #5……A RECALL ON VAGISIL

In my best angry old lady voice, I called the store knowing the assistant manager on duty would answer.

"Hello, my name is Reba, and I have a complaint, so I want to talk to the manager on duty". I grumbled in my best angry old lady voice.

"This is John may I help you?" "Yes, my vagina and lady parts are on fire after using the vagisil that I bought in your store." I said still projecting a louder tone of anger. "I'm sorry mam, I can give you a refund." John's voice trying to calm the old lady down.

"I don't want no dang refund; I want an incident report written up and I want to go to the emergency room." Don't you understand my vagina is on fire!" Trying to act like I was crying into the phone. "I'll get an incident report," John stuttered as silence fell on the phone.

Just seconds later John was back on the phone, and I was giving him my Reba Magilacutty (Not her real name) information complete with a fake phone number and address.

"Do I need to come to the store so you can take a few photos to turn into your insurance company?" I grumbled into the phone trying to be coy and sexy at the same time. "Or maybe you just need to see how red my vagina is?" Holding back my laughter with all my might.

"NOOOOOO mam, I don't need to take any photos, and I don't need to see how red your vagina is mam." John's voice was now trembling, and I could tell he was now trying to hold back his own laughter. I could no longer control myself and started laughing so hard tears were rolling down my face.

"You got me boss, I thought it was a real complaint, and that old lady voice had me fooled."

At one time pranks or practical jokes at work were commonplace and everyone needed a good laugh from time to time. Today practical jokes are a rarity.

JOKE #6……MANS BEST FRIEND…REALLY?

One rainy morning before the store opened, I noticed a small, scruffy looking puppy walking up and down the sidewalk as if he were lost. When

I opened the door and looked out, he came running up to me, wagging his tail as if he had just found a long-lost friend.

I petted him, dried him off and grabbed a box of dog biscuits from the shelf. He was cute and knew how to stand on his back legs and beg for a biscuit. While I was getting ready to open, I let him run freely around the store. Big mistake!!

I heard two of my friends and fellow workers calling me to the produce department where there was a large pile of dog poop!! I had no one to blame but myself for letting him run free and not paying attention to what he was doing.

Chuck and Ronnie stood in the aisle laughing, waiting for me to clean up the pile. I wondered how such a small dog could leave such a large pile of poop. I grabbed a roll of paper towels and a bottle of sanitizer and walked over to the mess. "Bad dog," I said with a little bit of anger thrown in. I started dropping sheets of paper towels on the mess and my friends kept the laughter flowing.

I figured as big as the mess was, I would have to use at least ten sheets. I reached down grabbing the paper towels and working the poop back and forth to get all I could up on my first try. When I picked the towels up there was nothing there and my friends were laughing even harder. It was fake poop!! I had been tricked. Well done, Chuck and Ronnie well done.

JOKE #7......FLOUR FIGHT, OR IT'S SNOWING IN CRYSTAL RIVER

This could have been a scene from the Three Stooges, Loell &Hardy or even a Charlie Chaplin movie. Nothing breaks the boredom better than a good old flour fight. A fight that leaves everything covered with a layer of whiteness that only a winter snowfall or blizzard could create.

Back in the day all grocery trucks were unloaded onto a roller/conveyor system that ran from inside the truck, through the backroom where four or five stock clerks separated the merchandise onto carts according to aisle. It was never a pretty sight when a case of cooking oil or ketchup fell off the roller and broke, what a mess. (during that era everything was glass not plastic like today) It was even worse when a bale of flour was accidentally ripped open, and its contents were scattered through the backroom.

What started out as a typical bale of flour being caught on the rollers and ripped open soon became an incident that legends are made of. A little flour jokingly flicked into a clerk's face led to retaliation where more flour was flung through the backroom hitting other clerks. Before you knew it everyone unloading the truck was throwing hands full of flour at each other. Before long there was no spot in the backroom that wasn't touched by

Pillsbury self-rising flour. The backroom was now a winter wonderland including clerks that looked like ghosts from Christmas past.

In walks Murry, the store manager and without hesitation says, "clean this mess up". Turns around and walks out of the backroom as if nothing really happened!

No write ups, no disciplinary action, no one was fired or suspended, it was back to work, business as usual.

STORY 15

CHRONIC TARDY SYNDROM; MAKES A CHIMP INCOMPITENT

If you're not ten minutes early, you're late. That's the consensus in the business world. The easiest task your boss will ever give you is for you to be on time and follow the schedule.

I'm not talking about being a few minutes late occasionally or a half an hour late because of an emergency. I'm talking about those that can't be to work on time on an almost daily basis. Employees that might show up an hour or more late with no good excuse. A hard-working employee that has that one fault. Getting to work on time.

Is that employee worth keeping around? An employee that causes others to miss part of their break or wait to go to lunch or even work later than scheduled to cover their shift.

That chronically late person can't be trusted to ever show up on time, although that may be his or her only flaw, is he worth keeping. You can't trust them to complete a time sensitive project on time. You can't trust them to open in the morning because they will keep your customers, vendors and other employees waiting. In retail you don't have time to wait for someone you can't trust to be at work on time.

You must document this person's tardiness because you know that sooner or later you will have to terminate that individual regardless of his other qualities.

Over the years I have lost more than one individual for chronic tardiness. Those are the people you hate to lose, the ones that work hard and do anything you ask but just can't be on time.

STORY 16

ANGER IS A GOOD CHIMPS ENEMY

Many people believe that anger is strength. They believe anger is power and are willing to use it to achieve their goals.

Those people are wrong, anger is a weakness. It clouds good judgement, causes mistakes and most importantly it pushes people away. Nobody wants to work with an angry person, and nobody wants an angry boss.

Anger suppresses new ideas, destroys trust, creates turnover and builds a wall between management and the people it depends upon to get the job done. There is no room for anger in any organization.

It's okay to show disapproval or concern but never show anger. It's also okay to be passionate about one's work but there is a thin line between passion and anger. Beware that your passion doesn't come across to your people as anger.

Anger destroys teamwork, enthusiasm, people's confidence, pride, punishes the people you care about the most and anger kills creativity.

If you find yourself always angry about something, it is time to make a change. Counting to ten also works and sometimes you just need to walk away.

STORY 17

MR. PERFECT: NO CHIMP IS PERFECT

Have you ever worked for Mr. Perfect? I have. The Mr. Perfect I once worked for was only perfect in his own mind. His management style was led by intimidation. Delegate everything so if it were wrong, he didn't get any heat from upper management. It was someone else's fault. He didn't know how to do anything so he couldn't teach you how to do it or even show you how it's supposed to be done.

He was one of those managers that was always in a bad mood and always on the lookout for other people's mistakes or shortcomings. He never told his staff they did a good job or shared the pat on the back he often received from other people's hard work. If you had done a great job, it just about killed him to tell you how great it was.

He was so predictable you could tell what kind of a day it would be the minute you saw his face when you walked into the store. The best days at work were his days off or when he was on vacation. When he made the schedule, he always made sure he had the best people during his shift and usually scheduled more people than he needed, always leaving his assistants understaffed, making it harder for them to get the job done. He didn't know how to lead by example.

On his first day back from vacation he always made it a point to knit-pick everything in the store so he could report to the DM what a mess the place was in and that he would fix it. He was so insecure he couldn't stand the fact the store ran better without him.

That was the beginning of his downfall. He didn't know his bosses were in the store the evening before his return, praising everyone for what a great job they had done while Mr. Perfect was on vacation.

The next morning when he started calling his bosses telling them what a mess the store was in, they responded, "How could it be in a mess? We were just there last night!" Upper management was beginning to see the real Mr. Perfect.

Within a few short months his management style or his one man show, began to fall apart. His associates started going over his head and Mr. Perfect was soon dismissed from the company.

The moral of the story is "YOU ARE ONLY AS GOOD AS YOUR PEOPLE" and if you don't believe that you have no place in management.

STORY 18

NO WORRIES, MATE: CHIMPS DON'T FREAK OUT

Retail management has literally hundreds of things that can stress you out. Hiring and firing employees, achieving required man hours and payroll, cash and inventory control, writing schedules, satisfying customers, achieving weekly sales projections, visits from corporate and a host of other intangibles can drive a store manager crazy.

One of my biggest stressors was getting the store ready for inventory. I always started preparing several days in advance but the night before I lay awake wondering if I had forgotten anything. I tossed and turned most of the night and when I finally did fall asleep, I would dream crazy dreams like Mac Davis the songwriter/actor was the inventory crew chief and was too busy walking around the store flirting with all the ladies and singing Baby don't get hooked on me, not paying attention to my inventory! Another dream I had was fighting giant snakes trying to keep them from eating all my inventory and my staff. Once mercenaries invaded the store running out the back door with carts full of merchandise. Any way you want to look at it, inventories are stressful.

Reaching my required sales per man hour was another stressor and it was a weekly thing. Most weeks I was busy getting my butt chewed out by the DM for missing my man hours, but I would much rather get chewed for that than bad store conditions.

Preparing for a corporate visit could also be stressful but I loved them. It was a chance to show off my store and my people. I always went the extra mile trying to make everything perfect. Corporate was some sixty miles away and didn't visit very often so I wanted them to have a good visit and leave happy. After all, to them you were only as good as your last visit and if it were bad that is how they remembered you.

The most stressed out I've ever been over a visit was Bill Thrift, our ROS and my DM Mike Prugh, were coming to take me to lunch. Other than an occasional lunch with my DM I had never had lunch with someone from corporate. And I was nervous about it.

I sat fidgeting in the back seat of Mr. Thrift's company car on the way to a local restaurant, not saying a word. We went into Fat Boy's BBQ and were immediately seated,

so far so good. We ordered and the waitress brought our drinks to the table. I was still trying to make small talk although I could feel the awkwardness of the situation.

My large, iced tea sat on the table beside me and I was so nervous I poured coffee creamer into it. An embarrassing mistake but we all laughed, and the waitress brought me another. My mistake lightened the mood, and the rest of the lunch was enjoyable. He had driven all the way from Orlando to Crystal River to congratulate me for my store's sales and ask if I would be interested in moving closer to Orlando. No was my answer and I was truly grateful to be invited to lunch.

STORY 19

CHANGE IS A FACT OF LIFE; CHIMPS MUST ADAPT

Change is a constant in all walks of life, nothing ever stays the same. The business world is no exception and if you are in the food industry, you must make more adjustments than most. Billions are spent every year in attempts to prepare management for change. To be successful in today's market, management must embrace change as if it were a close friend and do what is necessary to be a forerunner in the business world. During my first five years I worked for four different store managers. All were good men, and I was lucky enough to learn a lot from each of them before I was promoted to run my own store.

My first store manager was all about training and job placement. Picking the right person for the right job. Everyone has a different talent you just have to look for it. That made a lot of sense as some folks just aren't cut out to do certain jobs. His teachings gave me a strong base for job placement and the importance of good training.

The second store manager taught me merchandising and how to build a store that functioned like a family. Three or four times a year we had a store picnic at the lake and even a Superbowl party at his home. The employees viewed each other as family, and we always got the job done. While he was our manager, we were also number one in Sales per man hour for the entire division. Cross merchandising was his strong point and promoting high profit items.

My third store manager was undoubtably the smartest store manager I ever met. He taught me how to buy in inventory, the importance of keeping good records and staying on top of my daily bookwork. He taught me how to hire good people and sadly how to fire them as well. He let me handle the daily routine of running the store, making orders and schedules and handle employee discipline if necessary.

I was pretty much running the store when my fourth store manager arrived. He taught me not to be so hard on people. He taught me how to laugh and he reminded me that you get more from a horse with an apple than you do with a whip.

For the next fifteen years I was the store manager of the same store. I knew every customer by name, and they knew me. I realized my store was an important part of the

community so I supported all their projects and helped where I could. I supported the local schools, all their teams and all the teachers. It was a great town and WD was their store.

I learned something from every store manager I ever worked for, and they made me the manager I am today.

Several members of upper management came to visit from the corporate office. One of the VPs from corporate stated, "I love your management style, it's a style that can't be taught in a class. It comes from experience and putting different management styles together and making them work as one".

STORY 20

THE WELL-DRESSED CHIMP

During the sixties and even the early seventies if you were a stock clerk you dressed professionally in a white shirt and tie, black pants, shined leather shoes. And you were well groomed. If you were a part-timer at Winn-Dixie, you were issued a maroon bowtie and if you were full time, you wore a maroon business tie.

It didn't matter if you worked for Winn-Dixie, Publix, A&P, Kash&Karry or even an independent grocery company like Goodings or IGA stock clerks were considered professional and you had to dress the part.

Cashiers wore a dress uniform and were also expected to be well groomed. Dresses had better not be more than two inches above the knee either.

Stock clerks carried a jack stamp complete with holster, their case cutter and a feather duster stuck in their back pocket, as well as a roll of scotch tape in case they had to repair a torn label on canned goods or tape the top of a cereal box closed.

Sometimes we would have races to see who could price a case of canned vegetables faster than anyone else. Or pretend it was the old west and see who the quickest draw was getting their jack stamp out of the holster first.

During those days we worked hard and yes, we played hard too.
LOOK SHARP, DRESS SHARP AND BE SHARP

STORY 21

PAPA CHIMP ALWAYS GUARDS THE COMMUNITY

I always liked hiring a police officer's wife or girlfriend because when she worked late, he was always in the parking lot making sure she was safe. In turn anyone lurking in the area, up to no good, usually left and in the back of their minds my store wasn't a good place to cause trouble.

About ten minutes before closing time, I always made it a point of walking around the store. Checking refrigeration, looking around to see how many customers were still in the store and I would even check the restrooms to see if they had been cleaned, had supplies and if anyone was hiding.

When I returned to the front, I would lock both doors and let customers in and out as they came up front. This way I knew exactly how many people were in the store and anyone outside the store knew management was up front and vigilant for any wrongdoing.

I was happy to walk both customers and cashiers to their car after closing because you can never be too careful.

I would always notice unfamiliar cars in the parking lot after hours and sometimes I would call the police to check it out. Once the car had been stolen just a few hours earlier and left abandoned.

In any event it is always wise to know what is going on at closing time.

STORY 22

STAY ON SCRIPT, BUT I WANT MORE! WHAT'S HAPPENING CHIMPS

There are companies in the industry that do not want you to be creative when it comes to merchandising. They want you to stay on script and only on script. While an industry giant was interviewing me the interviewer asked me what I thought my strong points were. "Merchandising", I replied with a smile on my face, because I felt I was a master merchandiser. I won many National, State and company merchandising/display contests during my career. Cross merchandising always brought extra sales and adding a weekly push item was always a great sales increasing tool.

When my interviewer replied that her company didn't look upon merchandising as much of a strength I almost fell out of my chair. "You have to stay on script, and we will do the merchandising for you, don't do anything extra" she said without so much as a smile.

I knew how to stay on script because that was first and foremost. You must back the advertised items and place them in a convenient location for the customer. Also push items that corporate had committed themselves to push for various companies had their own special place, but they were missing the intangibles. Customers were in your store with money! They were there to spend it and to buy things, and it was my job to get that extra dollar from them. If I could get an extra dollar from every customer that came into the store that could be a few extra thousand dollars a week in sales.

I built tree houses full of pineapples, giant ships of beer or fruit juice,

Empire state buildings full of light bulbs, space shuttles overlooking mountains of cheese, talking Halloween candy displays, gorillas having cookouts, gorillas and giant bean stalks on the sidewalk promoting plants, Darth Vader and Yoda selling beer or pushing deli items. I even had giant watermelons as big as your car pushing watermelon season and Swiss girls along with the peanuts gang selling cheese. And if you can believe it I had the Easter Bunny selling plants on the sidewalk.

I ordered ten thousand dollars' worth of cheese for a massive cheese display and within two weeks I sold every bit of it. An extra ten thousand dollars the store had gotten in sales. Without it, zero dollars extra. Selling fifty cases of fresh pineapples, selling hotdogs and soda on the sidewalk, sampling donuts or cookies throughout the store and pushing items

on the intercom always boosted sales. I even had Wonder Bread's, Freddie the Fresh Guy come into the store on Saturday mornings and push bread and hand out free mini loaves of Wonder bread.

When I received free toys, flash cards, Jello or cake molds, candy, cookies or any other item I made a point of standing at the entrance door giving them away to customers as they walked into the store. This was a great way to meet my customers and for them to know who the store manager is.

Every week when I received the upcoming week's ad, I started making plans to go above and beyond whatever corporate wanted. Each store is different and must be merchandised according to its clientele. Not all stores can sell a pallet of fresh collard greens in one day and not all stores can sell a hundred cases of beer or soda in one day. Make plans for whatever works best in your store.

Never be afraid to try something new while pushing for extra sales. But when you do you have to give it your best shot. You must have commitment and if something isn't working you must adjust to make it work. Never, ever give up because you can do it.

STORY 23

KEEPER OF THE GATE; CHIMPS TAKING CARE OF BUSINESS

Other than your customers the most important group of people in your store isn't your store manager nor is it one of his assistants. It isn't the department heads, the office personnel, the stock clerks or delivery team. It's the person or group of people that have the hardest job in the store. This group of individuals can make or break your store. This group of people should receive the best training, get more pay than stock clerks and deserve more recognition than any other group of people you employee.

If you haven't guessed it yet it's your cashier team. They are your business's front line of defense for everything going on in your operation. Your good inventory results are literally in their hands. They see every customer that enters or leaves your store. They are your business's best PR system because they encounter more customers during their one-day shift than the store manager might in a whole week.

Why do I believe the cashier has the hardest job in the store?

1. They are responsible for all the monies collected in their till.
2. They are responsible for accepting all forms of currency whether it be cash, food stamps, WIC, SNAP and other vouchers as well as all forms of coupons.
3. Making sure the advertised items are ringing up as they should.
4. Making sure customers' orders are separated properly.
5. Making sure items are rang on the proper department.
6. Keeping their station clean and neat.

7. Proper bagging procedures followed. Cold items together, chemicals separated from perishables ect.
8. Help provide good front-end security.
9. Give great customer service as the cashier might be the only contact the customer may have with store personnel during their shopping experience.
10. Most importantly be able to satisfy the most unreasonable of customers while keeping a smile on their face and projecting the customer is always right image.

STORY 24

CUSTOMER SERVICE MANAGER, HEADCASHIER, MAMA CHIMP

There is one person in your store that is in the know about everything that's happening in your operation. It isn't the store manager, the DM or some fancy suit watching from the corporate Ivory tower. It's your customer service manager or head cashier. Those people know more than your nosey neighbor or one of your well-informed relatives. They know who is doing what, they know who your hardest workers are, who's slacking, who might be looking for another job or who your store troublemakers really are. They even know deep dark secrets.

The store manager is usually the last person to know anything because employees are simply afraid to share info with him. They feel he might be judgmental or overreacted with anger. They feel he might cut people's hours or even fire them and most people don't want that. They just want him to fix the problem.

Almost everyone comes to the customer service manager or head cashier with a problem before they will anyone else. I've always been amazed how many young people come to her with personal problems or advice before they will their own parents. The customer service manager or head cashier seems to be a problem fixer.

The customer service manager or head cashier is like an in-store HR department Counseling employees that need it. Sometimes she even takes on the roll as store psychologist.

BILL LANGSTON

When I was a store manager, I found myself listening to my customer service manager or head cashier on many occasions. They always knew what they were talking about and usually offered good advice. No manager is an island and depends on good people to help navigate troubled waters.

STORY 25

DON'T BE A SEAGULL; SMART CHIMPS KNOW HOW TO BE A LEADER

A smart leader knows the importance of motivation. He knows how to rally the troops and knows his subordinates are hungry for good advice and knowledge. He knows good communication is the key to all things and if you don't have good communication skills, you will never reach the results you desire.

THE HANDS-ON LEADER......I always admired the hands-on leader. He takes his coat off, rolls up his sleeves and jumps right in, physically helping fix whatever the problem may be. This leader, always leads by example, always teaching and training his subordinates. He always looks for the good and never hesitates to give praise or say, thank you, for a job well done.

Tell me......First he would tell me and explain the best way to accomplish whatever task it may be.

Show me......He would also show me how to do the task by example.

Do it......Then he would do it, showing me the best way to get the job done.

THE DELEGATING LEADER......This leader has great knowledge but chooses to delegate the job rather than teaching and showing ways to get the best results. In the event of failure, he always had a scapegoat. This leader usually never gets his hands dirty but stands back while others do it. Usually leads by using intimidation.

THE SEAGULL SUPERVISOR......At one time or another we have

all had this type of leader. A supervisor that swoops in out of nowhere, only pointing out the things that were wrong with your operation. "This is wrong, that's wrong, fix this, don't do that, what were you thinking, why did you do that, OMG, WTH". You know the drill. This supervisor seldom gives directions, advice, teaches or offers any suggestion on how to fix the problem and never gives praise or a pat on the back. The words, "Thank you," are not in his vocabulary. He just swoops out like he came but leaving his negative comments behind, expecting you to clean up whatever mess he might have left behind.

STORY 26

BEST JOB IN THE STORE; CHIMPS IN THE FAST LANE

It doesn't matter what position you hold in retail; somebody else's position may look easier with fewer responsibilities and not as many headaches but don't be fooled. All positions come with attachments and their own spare luggage.

Some positions are very physical, leaving you physically exhausted at the end of day. Some are mind boggling, keeping you mentally drained. Other positions may try your patience and leave you empty. Regardless, at the end of the day you must be patient and have your own plan for achieving the position you want. Don't be surprised if when you get it, it's not what you expected.

Being a clerk, you might think the guys in the meat department have the best and easiest job in the store. Every time you see the meat department gang they are on break. Eating donuts and drinking coffee as if they were a lone police officer on a stake out, killing time, waiting for action but best of all they are walking the meat case flirting with the pretty ladies. Who in their right mind wouldn't want that job?

Think again. Working in a meat room with the thermostat set just above freezing for eight hours or more isn't that much fun. Having to walk into the meat cooler just to warm up is a way of life for meat cutters. Everyday their feet get so cold they worry about frostbite as if they were stranded somewhere in the Alaskan Yukon. To top it off they must leave the cold meat room and go outside to unload a truck while working up a sweat. Then back to the freezing meat room to unload pallets of meat where some cases weigh more than one hundred pounds. A never-ending cycle.

Yes, it may look easy, but it comes with attachments. The smell of the trim barrel, being cold all day, the constant hustling to meet deadlines, dealing with product quality and one on one customer service. Like the song says, It don't come easy.

STORY 27

RED ALERT; BATTLE STATIONS......
DOUBLE COUPONS

Double coupon Sunday was nothing less than a hard, day long battle for sales. It was a no holds barred fight to the finish with the customer winning the battle for savings.

My stock crew worked all night, and the other departments stayed late the night before and came in early just to be customer ready. Everything was picture perfect on Double coupon Sunday mornings.

The floors look as clean and smooth as freshly polished glass. The grocery shelves were filled and finessed with pride and the weekly specials well stocked and displayed in every aisle. Extra bread was baked along with pies, cakes and cookies. Fried chicken, potato salad and sliced meats were ready for all shoppers. Ribs and a variety of steaks and roasts were filled, and backups were stored in the meat cooler waiting their turn to be taken home by bargain minded customers. Fresh and full was the produce department looking as if all the fruit and vegetables had just been handpicked from the Garden of Eden. All four corners of the store were perfect.

All the outside vendors left extra product in the backroom knowing when they returned there would be nothing left.

There was a cashier for every register scheduled all day long with a bagboy standing beside her. Knowing when I made the schedule there would barely be time for them to take a break or go to lunch. Double coupon Sunday was a day where it was all hands-on deck. Be ready to work hard from the minute the store opens until it closes. It was a day where you would be both physically and mentally drained.

Customers usually started waiting on the sidewalk about a half hour before opening time and it was common for twenty-five to thirty shoppers to be standing there with coupons in hand. It was a long hard day from beginning to end.

When we closed the store Double coupon Sunday evening it was destroyed. The shelves were bare, the specials in all departments were wiped out. You stood at one side of the store and looked with amazement at how the floors looked as if a herd of buffalo had stampede through the aisles. You and your staff were exhausted, worn out. Store sales usually doubled or even tripled on double coupon Sunday. WOW!! What a day!

STORY 28

COOKIE MONSTERS AND MILE HIGH KEY LIME PIE

EXCITEMENT was my greatest intangible asset. Motivating my team and keeping them excited always made a difference in everything we did. And there is nothing that makes a store manager happier than for his associates to come up with ideas to promote sales.

Every Thursday afternoon it was routine business to attend my DM's weekly sales meeting. We discussed previous week's sales, discussed the upcoming ad and our plans to maximize sales, we even discussed the much-dreaded topic of man hours. Everything we discussed was routine and kind of cut and dry without much excitement being generated.

I decided to fill my Monday staff meeting with excitement even giving away door prizes for best weekly sales increase and customer service recognition. I challenged my department heads to brainstorm with their associates for sales ideas and let them know I was willing to try anything if it motivated my people to push for sales.

The mile high key lime pie push for bakery sales was one of my bakery associates' ideas. Starting with the Saturday lunch time rush we announced every five to ten minutes the bakery had "MILE HIGH KEY LIME PIE" ready to take home for tonight's dessert. We sold more than fifty pies in just five hours. The bakery won the sales increase prize of the week. Two tickets for the new Batman movie! Everyone was jumping onto the excitement train.

Mr. Produce manager was the next to come forward wanting to sell fifty cases of pineapples. That Saturday all my employees were invited to wear Hawaiian shirts and leis to promote the sale of pineapples. From time to time, we would play a little Don Ho music between intercom announcements. Yes, the party was rocking the house.

The bakery was on fire and the bakery manager told me one of her people wanted to bake one thousand cookies the next weekend and sample them around the store and even on the sidewalk. COOKIE MONSTER was in the house.

The deli pushed fried chicken, potato salad and the meat department pushed Baby Back ribs and that Saturday the employees dressed in their best cowboy outfits including boots and country music filled the store. My store was on fire with excitement.

I discovered by using employees' ideas it gave them a feeling of ownership and magic was created between worker and company. My team and I dubbed ourselves as

THE SELLING MACHINE!

STORY 29

MOONLIGHT MADNESS OR WILD WEDNESDAY SALES

Moonlight Madness or Wild Wednesday sales!! I loved them. Corporate would always put extra money into advertising with special ads and the Division office always threw in a little extra incentive money or some kind of sales contest to make things interesting.

I kept my own special file with the phone numbers of most of my customers. They were regular customers with large families that spent a lot of money every week. School teachers, police officers, construction workers, Doctors, Lawyers, Realtors and even the mayor and city politicians were included in my list of customers to call.

The Moonlight Madness sales usually started around 6:00 PM on Wednesday evenings. Somewhere around 3:00 PM I would have one of my best customer service people start making phone calls to all the customers on my list. Reminding them we had a Moonlight madness sale tonight with many extra items on sale.

On Wild Wednesdays I would have phone calls made early on Tuesday evening inviting them to our Wild Wednesday event which usually had a whole page of deep cut specials to entice our customers.

I never got any negative feedback from the customers we called. Most of them were grateful for the call and many of them came shopping. If I had had any customer that was angry because we didn't call them, I would apologize, take their number and promise they would be the first customer I called for the next event.

Remember this was small town America and we were all neighbors. I knew them by name and they in turn knew me. I made my store their store and did whatever it took to keep them happy.

STORY 30

CLEANUP ON AISLE SIX; CHIMPS HATE TO CLEAN UP A MESS

"Oh Crap," could be heard from three aisles over when a clerk accidentally dropped a jar of pickles, but the applause he received from the other clerks could be heard across the entire store!

Plastic sure makes the modern stock clerks' job so much easier. When one accidentally dropped a glass bottle of cooking oil there was a ninety nine percent chance it would break today with a plastic bottle, the odds it will break are only fifteen percent.

Cooking oil was the worst mess ever. First you had to get the glass up, then pour kitty liter or salt over the entire oily mess. Sometimes you had to repeat the process several times before the floor was safe to walk on again. A cooking oil mess made everything slick, and it was a lawsuit waiting to happen.

My own personal stock crew tragedy was turning over a whole pallet of Thrifty Maid ketchup in glass bottles. It gave a whole new meaning to CRIMSON TIDE or RED SEA! It took hours to clean the mess up, but it still wasn't as bad as my first in-store cleanup.

My first cleanup as a bagboy was terrible. An elderly woman shopping by herself had just entered the store's lobby. She immediately started towards the restroom located at the back of the store, but she had waited too long. She started pooping up front and left puddles all the way to the lady's room. There was no hazardous waste protocol back then, only a mop bucket. No machine that I could just run over the mess to make the job easier. I heaved and gagged until I thought that I would throw up.

BILL LANGSTON

I've had friends turn over pallets of milk or drop cases of wine even turn the mop bucket over. But the one thing us bagboys hated more than anything was the dreaded call over the intercom system, "CLEAN UP IN AISLE SIX!"

STORY 31

THIS IS MY STORE; SMART CHIMPS TAKE OWNERSHIP

While I was the store manager of any store, regardless of whatever company I was working for I looked upon it as my store. I took ownership and operated it as if I owned it.

Of course I used the corporate guidelines in the day by day, routine operation. But it was my store, whether it was a good day or bad day, I was its captain. All the things happening were under my watch and it was my responsibly for its success or failure.

No man is an island, and no man can operate a store by himself. Always surround yourself with good people that take ownership with you, and it becomes our store. Make sure they are well trained, and you set them up for success. They too will have the store's best interest at heart. There is a certain amount of pride that comes with ownership. A new car, a new home or boat, or any other property you may possess. Taking ownership of your store is no different.

Whatever happens within the four walls of your store, good or bad as the manager you own it. It's yours and accepting responsibility for it is all part of the job. I've heard members of upper management make quotes like, "it's in the man, not the land" or "so goes the manager, so goes the store." There is truth in both of those quotes and the number one factor of any place of business is the quality of management. The best managers take ownership and make things happen. They don't just stand by and let things happen or get caught saying to themselves, "what happened?"

I was told as a young child that "Life is what you make it, not what other people make it for you". That is probably the best piece of advice I was ever given, and I pass it along to others as often as I can.

STORY 32

PREPARING FOR THE STORM; STAY SAFE CHIMPS

Operating a retail establishment in Florida, especially on the coast during Hurricane season comes with its own set of headaches. Headaches and heartaches that can last for weeks, sometimes months, even years or in the worst-case scenario, a lifetime.

My heart goes out to anyone that had to brave hurricane force winds, flooding, the loss of property including their business or home. Even worse, those that suffered the loss of a friend or family member. Katrina, Andrew, Charlie, Hugo, Ivan, Donna and many more killer storms will never be forgotten.

For more than forty years I operated stores on the central west coast of Florida, north of Tampa but south of Cedar Key. That area must have been blessed while I was working there. I had to weather only one Hurricane. Hurricane Elena in 1985, was my nemesis. Although hurricane Elena never made landfall in Florida but lingered off the coast of Crystal River for forty-eight hours before changing direction and going to Biloxi Mississippi. It still delivered high winds, flood waters and power outages. Bad Hurricanes hit both north and south Florida, the east coast and west coast on numerous occasions. Elena was my one and only bout with Hurricane forces.

I started receiving phone calls from corporate giving me instructions for securing the store. Soon afterwards my DM showed up giving me more advice on the many precautions I needed to take for the upcoming storm. By noon a crew of workers arrived placing sheets of plywood over all the windows and glass doors. By late afternoon panic shopping had taken a toll on the store. No water, no bread, no batteries and many other necessities one needed to survive the tropical demon was sold out.

That evening, I informed my DM that my family and I would be weathering the storm in the store as well as several other Winn-Dixie families. We felt that staying in the store would be a lot safer than hunkering down in our homes. My Jr. assistant manager's wife was pregnant with their second child and welcomed the chance not to be home by themselves.

That way we could also keep an eye on refrigeration, restock the store and keep both DM and corporate posted on any damages. We also kept the back of the store open for first responders and let them shop for whatever emergency needs they had, including emergency needs for local citizens.

We restocked the store while our wife's fixed dinner and the kids' watched movies. (We rented VHS tapes during that era) Lawn chairs and sleeping bags were positioned in the backroom and breakroom area turning the event into a sleepover of sorts. The kids played games like hide and go seek and played with remote controlled cars. The adults stayed up all night chatting and peeking out the back door from time to time to get a quick glance of whatever devastation the storm was causing. The howling winds began to sound like someone had unleashed the "HOUNDS OF HELL" on our small community. You could barely see the trees bending and falling over through the blinding downpour of hot rain. A murky river flowed through the parking lot and the drainage ditches were overflowing causing the parking lot to disappear as if it were a small lake. With a flash of lightning and a nearby explosion the parking lot became as black as looking into an Abyss or a blackhole. The occasional flash of lightning was welcomed, giving us a glimpse of the nearby buildings, our cars and what kind of destruction we could expect when the morning came. The store generator kicked in and the blinding darkness was changed into silhouettes of light. We covered the frozen food and dairy cases with cardboard and all the meat cases had been pulled earlier and placed into coolers.

Miraculously at daybreak the power came back on but the howling winds still bellowed through the small town, rain kept coming in blinding sheets and water levels were still rising. The parking lot lake was getting bigger and deeper, and the murky river of rain flowed out into US 19.

All day the winds kept its relentless pace, the rains died as if the storm was leaving only to return with a vengeance. Darkness still hovered over us as if it were dusk instead of the middle of the day. Never losing phone service, I received a call from the Division office informing me the storm was a mere twenty-five miles off the coast headed my way. I told everyone hunkering down in the store and we moved into a backroom walk-in cooler and turned its power off. We were safe and figured we wouldn't have to stay there for a long period of time.

After a few hours we went to check out the situation but there was no change. Elena was still lurking just off the coast and getting stronger. A few more hours passed, and I get another call, Elena had made a loop and was headed west, away from us. Thank God.

During the early morning hours Elena was far away from our coast and headed in a more northernly direction taking her wind and rain with her. Everything on the west side of US 19 was flooded but we were lucky enough to be high and dry on the east side. I called

employees to come into work if they could and we opened the store at 9:am with a skeleton crew.

There was a silver lining in this hurricane. My Jr. assistant and his wife couldn't agree on a name for the new baby after arguing about it for months. Elena was chosen and when I hear her name, I remember how lucky we were.

I know there are many horror stories out there where the entire store or town was blown away, the roof ripped off or the front windows and doors imploded under horrific winds. All merchandise was lost from power outages and even worse, lives were lost. And my heart goes out to everyone involved in such an ordeal.

When I think about Elena, I thank God everyday and sigh with relief on how lucky we were to dodge a bullet. Things could have been so much worse.

STORY 33

THE ALPHA

"All rise," a respectful voice echoed from behind the podium located at the front of the banquet room. The haunting melody of the death march filled the silent room, and more than one hundred store managers stood to pay their respects.

A coffin with six store managers serving as pall bearers slowly made its way to the front of the room. The casket had a sign with large letters draped over it, making a profound statement, "RIP Jacksonville Division".

Howard Hess, the man behind the podium, casually asked for all in attendance to be seated as he requested a moment of silence for the fallen Jacksonville division. He then started a eulogy, emphasizing the greatness the once powerful division had possessed.

This was the first Davis Cup the new Orlando Division was a part of, and as a new division we were sending a message to the current champion of all things that were Winn-Dixie. We were the new kids, and we were here to WIN. The eulogy continued challenging all in attendance to give their best effort achieving maximum sales during Davis Cup week. Winning the Davis Cup was our Superbowl. The winner had bragging rights for the entire year and no other division could take away its greatness.

I was a rookie store manager, and that day was the first time I had ever heard of Howard Hess. Within a few months he would become my DM, inspiring me to achieve many goals for my store and within a few more months he became our divisional ROS. He was a smart and educated businessman. Probably the smartest person in upper management I would ever know. He expected quality and always had a humorous may to make a point instead of being hardnosed and judgmental.

Howard Hess was the people's champion and had a rare personality. He could walk with Kings but never lose the common touch. "RIP Mr. Hess"

STORY 34

THE ANGEL OF DEATH

Probably the best and the most stress-free job I ever had was working as a General Manager for Scotty's. Scotty's was like a Home Depot or Lowe's specializing in hardware, building and contractor supplies as well as home furnishings, appliances, lawn and garden items and virtually everything you may need for a DYI project.

Their manager training program left a lot to be desired and consisted mostly of helping to remodel and clean existing stores. But like I said, it was stress-free.

After working there for about two weeks the store manager found me working in the paint department and informed me the company president would be making a visit to the store sometime around 10:00 the next morning. I immediately thought to myself, "crap, we're going to be here all-night cleaning and finessing the store". At 6:00 pm a call over the intercom for me to come to the office gave me the feeling of more corporate news to reaffirm pulling an all-nighter so off to the office I headed.

To my surprise the store manager was ready to leave and said, "Bill, let's go home". In amazement I replied, "Isn't the president of the company coming in the morning?" The manager laughed saying, "yes, we swept the floor twice!" So out the door we headed. When the president arrived the next morning, he was in a festive mood, shaking everyone's hand, thanking all for a job well done and left without really inspecting the store.

Within the next few days, I was assigned to a store in Tarpon Springs as its new General Manager. I started training myself how to run a forklift, use various saws and spent time with the delivery driver learning the area. The store was filled with great employees that really loved the company and took pride in their jobs. Sadly, before the month was over an announcement was made making it common knowledge the company was in financial trouble and had started closing stores and liquidating assets. That was the beginning of my task of being assigned as General Manager of stores scheduled to be closed.

This was in the late nineties and there was a popular television show called, "Touched by An Angel," with one of the characters named Andrew which was the "Angel of Death".

Andrew would show up when it was time for someone to pass away and help escort them to the light or the hereafter.

When I would show up at a store the word of my arrival would spread like wildfire and the employees knew I was there to close their store. The whispering, "The Angel of Death is here", echoed through the store with the sadness of losing a dear friend.

I would help employees find new jobs and help where I could with getting unemployment benefits for those that needed them. After closing several stores, I left the company and within a few short years the company no longer existed. Truly a sad day.

STORY 35

SOMETHING NEW

Most people don't like change. They don't like to try something new in fear they won't like it or that new idea just plain out sucks. They may feel that something new might cause more work or more planning on their part. Many people will try to find numerous excuses as to why something new will fail and be a liability.

I have sat in many sales meetings with fellow store managers listening to them complain about trying a new idea. Listening to them gripe about something new causing extra hours that weren't built into the budget. The biggest reason is they just don't want to try. Even if it is as simple as making shelf space for a new item or trying to promote something corporate or the DM wants them to try.

One company I worked for started carrying a new chocolate cake and a new lemon cake at a reasonable price. Our DM had the idea for the store manager to hand deliver one sample cake to each store doing business in our shopping center. He had several reasons for giving our neighboring businesses a cake. Most of the managers in the meeting couldn't understand his reasoning, but I did.

1. It gave the manager the opportunity to meet his neighboring businessmen if he hadn't already done so. I for one had not met all my neighbors even though I had been there for several years.
2. It was a gift for them to put in their breakroom for their employees to enjoy.

3. It was a creative way to push a new product, that happened to be quality product. And create extra sales by possibly bringing new customers into the store.

I delivered a cake to each of my neighbors and got to meet people I had never met before. The cake was good, and I enjoyed the extra sales the DM's idea produced. I went from selling a meager case or two a week to where I had to build a display to keep up with the sales.

Remember when twenty-four pack beer was first introduced to the public. Almost every manager in the meeting complained about carrying the new product. I for one didn't because I saw its potential. The first weekend it hit the market I ordered six hundred cases for a massive lobby display. And guess what!! It sold!!

Corporate wanted four kinds of homemade fudge made in the deli and a massive display built. You guessed it. The negative minded started making every excuse imaginable as to why it wouldn't sell. But guess what. It was the deli's number one seller throughout the holidays.

Many store managers hated sidewalk sales, especially pushing produce on the sidewalk. Their philosophy was they have the same items inside so the customer could buy it there instead of the store wasting time putting the same items on the sidewalk.

Eighty percent of all produce items are impulse buys. In other words, eight out of every ten produce items a customer buys are not on their list. Quality and eye appeal are the key. If you just throw the product out there and don't make it look desirable it will not sell. You have wasted your time. But to make it look like they are at a freshly picked and displayed farmer's market makes all the difference in the world. So how many extra impulse sales did you pick up by having something new and exciting going on for your customers?

The moral of the story is, "IF YOU NEVER TRY, YOU NEVER KNOW" so be open-minded and give new things a chance.

STORY 36

MY WORKING FAMILY

When I think about yesterday, I think about you. I think about good times and bad times, and I remember all the things that brought us together. I remember going to work early and staying late. There were more hard days than easy ones. I remember we were closer than friends, we were family. Through the years we worked side by side with common goals. We never hesitated to help each other and when you needed us, we were at your side. And when your family at home needed us, we came running. We never hesitated to give a helping hand. We never let each other down.

There was no such thing as 9:00 to 5:00, from time to time we went to work before the sun was up and many times we stayed until after dark. We were there, side by side, and we stayed busy taking care of business. Nobody really understands the closeness we share or the ties that bind us. But it's there, this friendship, this comradery, this brotherhood all ties us together, we are FAMILY.

ACKNOWLEDGMENTS

There were many contributors for A CHIMPANZEE'S GUIDE FOR RETAIL MANAGEMENT. These contributors, friends and fellow workers, inspired me to do my best and I hope this book makes them proud. I enjoyed working with the many people mentioned below. I always viewed you guys as friends, never as employees or the boss.

David Kirby, Zola and Krissy Wagner, David and Patty Alsobrook, Jeff Endsley, Ken Clack, Hal Klopfer, Dan Lafever, Mike Prugh, Leon Stewart, Howard Hess, Phil Filosa, Mark Mclin, John Giddens, Dan Wynn, John Few, Duane Harvey, Tim Richards, Tom Goolsby, Jere Bedford, Chuck Clendenney, Ronnie Roddenberry, Mac Holmes, Gary Miller, Billy Wells, Ellis Ware, Jim Bradshaw, Phyllis Campbell, Gale Newsome, Roy Grace, Gary Finch, Cheri Holland, John Haas, Barbara Hoven, Judy Hoven, Debbie Hyde, Ann Marie McGee, Jerry Sapp, Pam Kelly, Mary Hessinger, Tom Miller, Dennis Bantz, Duane Finch, Bobby Wear, Larry Wilson, Judie and Tom Mathews, Tami Glover, George Buzby, Holly Amos, Jeanie Neil, Don Mullady, Denise King, Dave Hiley, Chris Carroll, Wayne Rolph, Jan Gathje, Bruce Ferguson, Susie Wong, Louise Siner, Dade Conger, Barbara Hughes, Chip DeClue, Jeffery Campbell, John Russo, Billy Hout, Gary Richards, Larry Blanken, Darryll Tyson, Kim McGee, John Sawn, Nan Baker, Robin Foster, Billy Dowling, Tim Fogarty, Homer Ryan, Bill Thrift, Diane McBride, Marion Coppens, Michelle Carraher, Norman Scriven, Mike Watkins, Harold Chandler, Tom Altier, Lou Martone, Greg McGreggor, Bill Phillips, Ralph Pietrobergo, David Berguristian, Bill Decker, Bill Moore, Debra Patrick, Joanie West, Renee Norcross, Crystal Plants, Pama Hardy, Clint Croft, David Moen, Todd Watson, Matthew Brown, Matthew Spate, Drew Phillips, AJ Cochran, Sharon Raynor, Dane Herb, Amy Woods, Rozina Jenkins, Dominic Willis, Jimmy Hessinger, Leon Mayes, Sue Terry, Mel Navas, Lafonda England, Kim Leach, Gene

Wear, Jimmy Wear, Jimmy Campbell, Fran Ritzenheimer, Ruth Sprague, Pat Regan, Tom Brooks, Bob Grimm, Jeff Lacoff, Terry Woodard, Don Martin, Jerry Popp and Jimmy Hanson.

"THANK YOU FOR ALL YOU DID"

Bill Langston, Bob Jones and Jim Bradshaw

the first of many promotions

Early 1960's Cash Register

Never Fear, If the power went out just put the crank

In the side for the bagger to turn and keep checking

out groceries

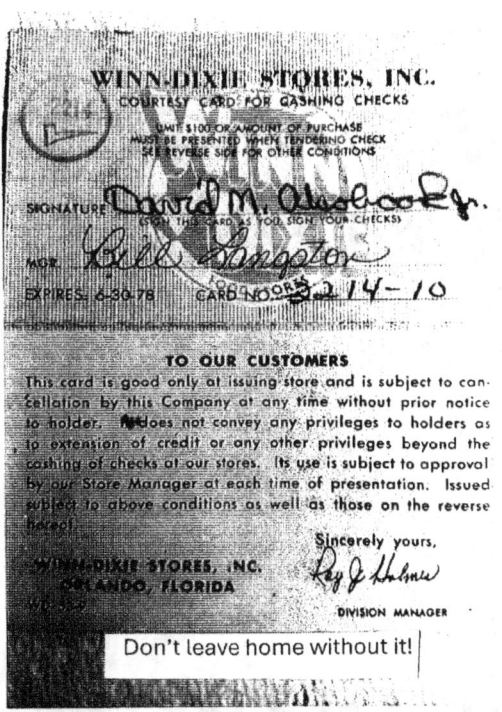

Don't leave home without it!

Keep on trucking

Bill Langston and DM Leon Stewart

Holly Amos sampling various types of Cheese for the Cheese Adds a Slice of Life Promotion at Store 2227

We won a nice cash prize
and #1 in the Florida Citrus
display contest with the
USS SUNSHINE

USS OLD MILWAUKEE

Hum, does Tarzan live here?

Great tropical fruit display. Sold fifty cases of pineapple and avocados in one weekend!!!!!!

BE COOL, DRINK CHEK SODA

Bonus money and Gold Rush Points

A stock clerk's weapon of choice

The Jack Stamp

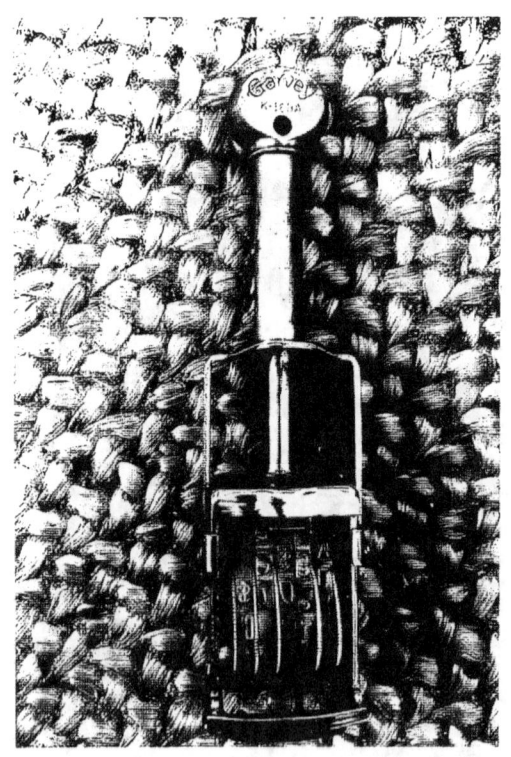

Bill Langston — Danny Woods DECA Coordinator

Employer of the year 1981, 1983 and 1985

Krissy and Zola Wagner
Store Party

My favorite day at work; Bring your daughter or granddaughter to workday

Lafever's Eagles

Commitment to Excellence

Winn-Dixie Produce Sidewalk Sale

Everybody loves a good Farmers Market

Our employees loved Harvest sales week.

Chuck Clendenny Roy Grace Bill Langston Mike Hagar Jimmy Campbell

Team #2227 in Crystal River Florida